THE SILENCE OF MY FATHER

Alexandre Najjar

The Silence of My Father

Translated from the French by
Laurie Wilson

TELEGRAM

ISBN: 978-1-84659-065-8

First published as *Le silence du ténor* by Plon
Copyright © Plon, 2006
Translation © Laurie Wilson, 2010
This edition published in 2010 by Telegram

A full CIP record for this book is available from the British Library.

Manufactured in Lebanon

TELEGRAM
26 Westbourne Grove, London W2 5RH, UK
2398 Doswell Avenue, Saint Paul, Minnesota, 55108, US
Verdun, Beirut, Lebanon
www.telegrambooks.com

To 'Mine'

Contents

'Your eyes would discover in my own all the protection you desire from that tall being with the deep voice that is called a father.'
Jules Supervielle, 'Gravitations'

'It is the orator for whom the disadvantages of old age are most to be feared.'
Cicero

Prologue

The day I was born, my father planted a cedar tree in the garden. That meant he loved me as much as his country.

Talking about one's father is always delicate; there is something immodest about it. My father is a novel character. He probably isn't the only one, given that most children believe their father is a hero. Mine was a lawyer in Beirut. After studying law with the Jesuits, he took over his cousin's firm, and thanks to his dedication, he managed to turn it into one of the most renowned in Lebanon. Being an expert in maritime law, his nickname was *Amir al-bihar*: the Admiral.

My father taught me a great deal. At once authoritarian and gentle, austere and mischievous, he was a teacher of hope.

Values

All his life, my father cultivated a passion for three things: his homeland, his work and his family.

His homeland? The Admiral never ceased to defend a certain idea of Lebanon. An 'independent, prosperous and cultivated' Lebanon, as his role model Charles de Gaulle asserted; a pluralistic Lebanon whose eighteen religious communities would cohabit in complete harmony. Born in 1923, just after the proclamation of the State of Greater Lebanon by General Gouraud, my father has lived through it all: the French Mandate, the Independence of 1943, the Belle Epoque (the fifties and sixties), the war, the occupation. In a way, Lebanon was his friend, his accomplice, his confidant, as he had accompanied it since its birth and witnessed all its trials and tribulations in this region of the Middle East that has never known peace. While very attached to the Land of Cedars, he was a Francophile and expressed himself as easily in French as he did in Arabic, though he rolled his 'r's. According to him, we were the descendants of a Corsican family: our ancestor, Joseph Damiani, had accompanied Bonaparte during his Egyptian campaign. Wounded at Saint Jean d'Acre, he was unable to resist the charms of a beautiful Lebanese woman, perhaps his nurse, and, in the name of love, decided to stay in the Orient. Just after his recovery, he settled in a village called Deir al-Qamar (Monastery of the Moon) where he worked as a carpenter. He was thus christened *Najjar*, the equivalent of 'woodworker' in Arabic. Was this a true story or did my father make it up in order to create common origins with the French Emperor? For a long time I believed the latter hypothesis, until I came across a book on Lebanese families attesting to the former.

The Admiral was a glutton for work, he was addicted to it. Law was more than a profession for him: it was a calling. Sitting at his desk in his office or at home, he would draft contracts and compose statements of reply from dawn until late into the night. Even on Sundays, the day of rest, he would bury himself in his files and would not leave his desk until close to midnight, his eyes heavy with sleep. He took pleasure in countering his adversaries' claims, patiently searched through the *Encyclopédie Dalloz* or old books which he referred to by their authors' names (*Houpin et Bosvieux, Escarra et Rault, Aubry et Rau, Ripert et Roblot* ...) for the references likely to reinforce his defence, drew upon important judgments from legal precedent, and always developed a clear outline in which the arguments were set out with implacable logic. At the age of three, when I was asked what he did, I would spontaneously respond '*Biéktob, biéktob*', which means 'He writes, he writes!' As long as he had a pen in his hand, my father did not feel the slightest fatigue. He was such a perfectionist that he wrote several rough drafts and only submitted drafts that were free of corrections to his typist. To justify this (but was that necessary?), he was forever citing the following witticism from Charles de Gaulle: 'I do four rough drafts. Only Flaubert outdid me: he did five!' Approached twice about becoming the Minister of Justice, he had refused this honour, under the pretext that 'politics is a waste of time'. For him, the legal profession was so sacred that all the laurels in the world could not have diverted him from it. The judges had great respect for him: I remember they would stand when he entered their offices and walk him to the door when he left. In their eyes, he symbolized competence, probity and experience. My father had begun his career pleading before the joint Franco-Lebanese courts. He belonged to the generation that had experienced the golden age of justice and had inspired President Charles Hélou to make the following enthusiastic statement: 'The Lebanese bar was so excellent that it was extremely difficult to make one's place among the star lawyers, all of whom were brilliant, cultivated, of superior intellect, with an equally profound knowledge of Arab and French cultures.'

At that time the court-house was located near the *Grand*

Sérail monument. The Admiral would walk there and, after his hearings, would gladly linger beneath the large oak tree that dominated the courtyard to talk with his fellow lawyers. His office was located near the port of Beirut, facing the sea. At the beginning of the war, in 1975, it was the target of several bombs, which ravaged part of its library. Taking advantage of a cease-fire, he went to the devastated building one morning to remove what could be salvaged. Under sniper fire, risking his life, he brought back boxes filled with scattered files, half-burned books. I can only begin to imagine the immense sadness he felt upon seeing the fruit of his labour in such a state ...

My father introduced me to the tricks of his trade very early on, hoping to see me take over one day. That is how, at the tender age of seven, I decided to become a lawyer. But what in the beginning was simple imitation gradually evolved into a profound conviction: injustice in all forms revolted me, and lawyers alone could defend the cause of victims in order to repair injustices. I thus became a lawyer and did my internship in my father's firm after studying law in Paris. This training period inculcated in me his integrity ('Our acts follow us,' he would repeat to me, claiming for his own the title of a book by Paul Bourget), but not in the least his military discipline, which was incompatible with my temperament. It taught me at least the following three lessons: always return to the source, to law texts; never give a client false hope; believe in the chances of winning a case right up to the end. 'Nothing is won or lost until you reach the finishing line,' he used to tell me. 'Being a lawyer requires a great deal of faith.' He had a gift for being concise in the contracts he established. One day he sent a draft of a settlement to a fellow lawyer concerning a tricky litigation that had already given rise to a dozen legal proceedings. Having received two pages on his fax machine, the lawyer thought there were some pages missing, and asked his secretary to call my father's office to ask for the rest of the contract. But at the last minute he changed his mind; everything was there. In four carefully written clauses, the Admiral had covered all aspects of the issue and made provision for every possible scenario. Unlike most lawyers who overload their conclusions with 'superfluous' defence mechanisms, the Admiral limited himself to serious means: 'I just can't help it,' he confided to me. 'If I'm not convinced by the arguments I put forward, my pen stops writing!'

My father's closing arguments fascinated me: no court-room theatrics, no prosopopoeia. To his fellow lawyers' lyrical flights of fancy he responded with legal – or 'scientific', as he used to say – arguments, following a carefully prepared strategy. His voice, strong and clear, resonated all the way into the waiting hall. During a case involving the assets of a business in which the opposing counsel – a distinguished university professor – had pleaded, gesticulating, for an hour, the Admiral was brief: from the folds in his robe he pulled the Commercial Law book written by his fellow lawyer and read a paragraph to the court. The chosen excerpt contradicted the closing argument. 'My distinguished colleague', said my father, 'is arguing the opposite of what he teaches at the university. This means one of two things: either he is misleading his students, or he is misleading the court. The court will weigh the evidence.' And the court weighed the evidence.

The Admiral was an idealist. He could not imagine that justice could be corrupt, nor could he tolerate the interference of executive power in legal affairs, even though Justice, having become 'a dressed-up form of vengeance' according to Stephen Hecquet's felicitous formula, often acted like a courtesan. I remember that the deplorable state of the magistrature after the war greatly saddened him: 'What a terrible shame!' he used to repeat to me every day, comparing the current state of justice to that of the past.

My father attached little importance to fees and devoted all his Saturdays to the various religious congregations that consulted him free of charge. When, following his example, I abandoned the idea of asking a poor client to pay my fee, he said to me, smiling: 'You're the Mother Teresa of the law profession', knowing perfectly well that my attitude was modelled on his own principles. A German saying goes: *Juristen, böse Christen* (Lawyers are bad Christians), as it is a well-known fact that charity does not carry much weight when it comes to strictly applying the law. As for the Admiral, he was an exception to the rule.

Family occupied a very important place in my father's heart.

Marrying late in life, at the age of forty-three, an exquisite woman – my mother – who was twenty-six, he made up for lost time: they had six children in four years, a feat that can be explained by the existence of two sets of twins within our tribe. Because of his work, Father was often away. When asked to draw his family, my youngest brother always drew him outside of the house. Yet, in spite of this distance, my father never gave us the impression that he was far from us. It is true that my mother's availability helped to fill the void, but he had a flair for attaching such importance to the rare moments of intimacy he granted us that they were enough to satisfy us. Americans often use the expression 'quality time'. That is exactly what it was. The morning kiss, the family prayer, the pre-bedtime 'good night' ritual that consisted of going into his room to receive a kiss and an affectionate pinch on the neck, and, above all, the moonlight walks on the balcony: my father would invite each of us in turn to accompany him during his nightly stroll. Lulled by the croaking of the frogs, beneath a starry sky, we would meander back and forth, talking. What did we talk about? About the future, our problems, ways to overcome them ... As a sign of affection, my father had the habit of resting his hand on the nape of our neck while walking. He had also chosen a nickname for each of us: I was *al-oustaz al-saghir* (the little lawyer) and my sister *bissé* (the kitten) because as a child she used to snuggle up to him like a little cat. No words can describe the bond that forms between a girl and her father. I know, having seen it in his eyes, all the love he felt for her. And I remember that on her wedding day, his eyes were swollen from having cried all night: he could not admit that my sister had grown into a woman in love, with the desire to build a life of her own far from the paternal bosom! There was also Fred Astaire (the youngest had earned this name by dancing at a party at the junior high school), Le Corbusier (one of my middle brothers dreamed of becoming an engineer), Leonardo (his twin, with a gift for painting) and Lyautey (my father hoped that the brother in question, unruly by nature, would be disciplined like the Marshal). These affectionate nicknames were his private ground. My mother never used them, nor did we for that matter. For my father, it was the best way to show us our uniqueness.

Family, in Papa's eyes, was to be understood in the larger, shall we say 'Mediterranean', sense of the word. The family circle was not limited to mother and children, but also included our great-uncle, great-aunt, uncles, aunt and cousins. My father, who was the youngest of five children, venerated his brothers and sister, and never missed an occasion to invite them or even to take them in during the war. Family lunches brought together some thirty people around his patriarchal figure.

In spite of the war, I had – I am not ashamed to admit – a happy childhood. In the country house my father had built shortly before I was born and where there stood an authentic Lebanese cedar, I accumulated memories. They come back to comfort me in times of despondency, as I see, with the passing of time, those I love wither or pass away.

Role Models

My father is very thin. As an adult he has always maintained the same weight, one hundred and thirty pounds. Contrary to the majority of Lebanese people who appreciate good food and have a belly, he has a flat – if not concave – stomach. According to an old passport he is five foot nine inches tall. He has dark hair, but it has been greying since he was sixty-five. His face is long, his forehead bare, with a dome-like stateliness. He has a dark complexion, a pronounced nose, protruding ears, and his eyes, framed by gold-rimmed glasses, are an undefinable colour, a mix of blue, grey and green. He has large hands, bony fingers, and on the tip of his right middle finger, a callous caused by the constant pressure of his pen. He has a habit of clearing his voice as the result of an allergy, the cause of which he has never known. When he smiles, his eyes light up, his cheeks wrinkle, a v appears on his forehead. But when he is unhappy, his face tightens, his expression becomes fearsome. His thin figure could be compared to that of Arthur Miller or the poet Georges Schéhadé. It does not match his temperament – that of a man of character. For my father has always been demanding of himself and of others. If we took second place in class rather than first, he called us 'Poulidor', in reference to a famous French cyclist who always finished second behind Jacques Anquetil. At the law office, he exhorted us to outdo ourselves, to delve into things ('You have to be a deep-sea diver,' he used to tell me), not to give in to easy solutions. He was forever asking Fred Astaire, who had become an economist, what the gold rate was, just to verify that he was 'up to date'. He reproached Lyautey, who was involved in numerous sports activities and daring adventures, for being 'whimsical'. In his eyes, we were always on probation, which, far from discouraging us, motivated us to push ourselves beyond our limits. Of course, we sometimes suffered from an unjust or hurtful word, but this was nothing compared to our desire to do better.

The Admiral liked to give us 'role models'. First there was Napoleon. He knew the Emperor's history by heart, could reconstitute all his battles and name all his generals. He even had an authentic copy of one of Napoleon's letters, dictated during the Italy campaign and signed with just the following three letters: 'Nap'. There was also de Gaulle who, in his eyes, was an exemplary being. He had named his youngest son Charles in honour of this role model and bought anything that was closely or remotely related to the life of the General, overdoing it to the point of subscribing to the magazine *Espoir*. A man of faith, of conviction, of character, de Gaulle had so captivated him that he had taken advantage of one of his rare trips to France to make a pilgrimage to Colombey-les-Deux-Eglises. He was also drawn to Marshal Lyautey who, in his opinion, had done an admirable job of governing Morocco. During his childhood he had been awarded the prize for excellence in history by the Jesuit priests, and for this had received a biography about this figure. These great men had one thing in common: they were true 'leaders'. In my father's eyes, this word said it all: 'leader'. It evoked at once will, self-possession, discipline and the ability to command. It is no doubt for this reason that he brought a baseball cap back to me from a trip to Paris, with an insignia that read, 'Follow the leader!' In giving it to me, he said, in a serious tone: 'Always be a leader!'

I kissed him, conscious of the heavy responsibility this cap suddenly placed on my shoulders.

These historical figures – Napoleon, de Gaulle, Lyautey – overshadowed all others for my father. Thus, the day he saw me, at the age of seventeen, wearing a t-shirt with Che Guevara on it, with his star-emblazoned beret and his cigar between his lips, he nearly fainted and ordered me to get the impious image out of his sight immediately.

Where literature was concerned, his intransigence manifested itself with the same intensity. For him, a student of Jesuit priests, only Hugo, Corneille, Racine and, closer to us, Daniel-Rops were worthy of interest. One evening he caught me reading a book by Camus – *The Plague* or *Caligula*, I do not remember which. How could I forget the disappointment that came across his face at that moment? He glared at me and said, bitterly: 'You should read more wholesome books!'

'But Father, it's Albert Camus!'

'Precisely: Camus is a subversive writer!'

'Subversive?' His quick judgment left me speechless.

All these 'role models' that my father handed down to me have stayed with me. Perhaps more glorious or humane role models exist, but his have the important feature of always reminding me of the advice he gave me that day, slipping the baseball cap onto my head: 'Always act like a leader!'

Paradise

Our house is strategically located in a spot where you can see both Mount Sannine and the town of Bikfaya at the same time. For my father, the clear view this place offers was its best feature: to avoid it being obstructed by anarchic construction, he didn't hesitate to buy the adjacent property. 'That way I have nothing to worry about,' he told my mother. The house, which consists of three stories and an attic, stands at the end of a lane lined with privets and paved with pebbles. The entrance is protected by a glass door; the steps leading to the front door are lit up by three wrought-iron lamps. Umbrella pines, oleanders, a stunted willow and a Lebanese cedar – mine – fill the garden. The lawn, which spreads out to the left of the entrance and continues all the way to the vast terrace where all our family meals take place in the summer, is brightened up by an immense flowerbed of rosebushes and huge mortars that have been transformed into basins: French marigolds, snapdragons and knotgrass flower there from May to October. Cats, hens, snails, frogs and butterflies have taken up residence in this natural habitat. In the middle of the lawn, a cement slab was poured to fill a deep hole. For a long time, I thought it was an underground passage that linked the house to the garden: I dreamed of taking it to go outside to play without arousing the suspicion of my parents, but was afraid it was infested with evil creatures and snakes. It was not until the age of fifteen that I learned the truth: although he was very Cartesian, my father had called upon the services of an old water diviner in the hope of digging a well which would serve to better irrigate the lawn. The nice man, who was more like a Native American shaman than a geophysicist, had prospected in the garden with the help of a divining rod and 'found' the location of the groundwater. For three months, a drill pounded its way into the ground in the spot that had been indicated. To no avail. My father did not admit defeat. He waited for three months and called in a more efficient machine. It was a waste of effort. The water witch had obviously mistaken the senile trembling of his hands for a movement in his divining rod. Grudgingly, my father ended up throwing in the towel. Though disappointed, he was able to maintain a sense of humour about it: 'If I had continued to dig, I would have reached the Cape of Good Hope!'

Below the lawn, the space is divided into two symmetrical parts: the vegetable garden and the orchard. Along the boundary there is a 'buffer zone' formed by an arbour laden with heavy clusters of red grapes. The stairway leading up to it has widely-spaced steps flanked with a double hedge of lavender – sachets of which my mother liked to put in with our laundry – where lizards come to bask and which squadrons of bees begin to storm every day at noon. The façade of the house, covered in ochre-coloured freestone, is not at all in the Oriental style: it has neither arcades nor *moucharrabié*,[1] but a balcony with a stylized banister and a gable hatched with wooden studs, just like the half-timbered houses of Alsace or Normandy. Only the orange-tiled roof, which tops the majority of traditional Lebanese homes, reminds visitors they are in the Levant.

Inside, the furniture is French, Italian and Chinese; the massive fireplace is topped with a shell-adorned sponge, an African drum and a pewter carafe. This eclectic decor does not give an impression of disorder, but rather gives the house a certain amount of character: the objects are chosen, each put in its place. Everything is *in order*.

My father loved his house. 'It's my paradise,' he always said to me when he opened the shutters and Mount Sannine, illuminated by the light of the setting sun, revealed itself to our gaze. He knew its every nook and cranny, every plant, every stone. In the summer, he liked to inspect the vegetable garden and the orchard, and carefully protected them from parasites. Every September, he called upon our services for apple-picking. Wearing sombreros, under the blazing sun,

---

1. A kind of bartizan that adorns Oriental palaces.

we industriously filled dozens of crates, which he stocked in a refrigerated warehouse in preparation for winter, so we could eat apples all year long.

One day, I resolved to plant strawberries in the garden and asked my father for permission to use a plot located near the cedar tree. He gladly accepted. But in spite of my efforts and my painstaking reading of gardening books, I only managed to get one seedling to grow which, in the end, bore only a single strawberry. Putting on a brave face, I picked it and, placing it in a saucer, offered it to my father who was having breakfast. Upon seeing it, the Admiral was careful not to mock my wasted efforts. He took the strawberry, put it on his tongue, then voluptuously let it melt in his mouth: '*Mnel jnainé*!' (It's from the garden!) he sighed, pinching my cheek.

Discipline

'*Yalla*,[1] athletes!'

My father woke us every morning at seven o'clock for our physical education class. Scantily clad and barefoot, we went into the living room and stood to attention. The Admiral took command. He stood facing us, as straight as an arrow. Then, 'one, two,' he began to count with an authoritarian voice, leading us in the movements. Upon his signal, without a word, all six of us performed the various exercises he had planned. It was nice outside. We could hear the gurgling of the rivulets and the chirping of the cicadas.

Why did my father insist so on our daily workouts? He had probably suffered as a child from being too skinny, less athletic than his friends, and wanted us to build strong bodies to save us from future sarcasm and humiliation.

As the eldest, I sometimes took over from him and led the physical education session that he imposed on us. So I

---

1. 'Let's get going' in Arabic.

could successfully carry out this thankless task, my father had entrusted me with a book written by a body-building champion whose name I forget. The book had several illustrations and promised its naive readers that in under three months they would look like the author, whose superior musculature was displayed on the cover. But in the end, while the exercises kept us in shape, they did not make athletes of us. We thus went through a period of doubt: all those tiresome sessions, all those daily sacrifices had been useless!

One day my father decided to sign me up for after-school track-and-field classes at the junior high school. I could protest all I wanted, tell him that I preferred football, it did not do any good: I found myself in the midst of pole-vaulters and discus throwers, incapable of keeping up with them, frustrated at being subjected to sporting events for which I was not cut out. The following year, the Admiral reluctantly decided to spare me this torture and finally allowed me to join the school football team. During my first game I tried my luck from afar and, with a strong kick, shot the ball into the opposing team's net. It was the only goal of the game. Pleased with my performance, the coach called my father to congratulate him. Coming to the realization that I was a talented football player, the Admiral gave up on making a decathlete of me for good.

My father ran our family like a general. A bit like Captain Georg von Trapp in the film *The Sound of Music*, he kept us in line, so well that guests who came to our house were surprised by the calm that prevailed in spite of the presence of half a dozen children. At lunchtime, discipline was strictly enforced. My mother rounded up her tribe by yelling, 'Children!' No sooner had she said that than her six famished offspring rushed down the stairs leading to the dining room. '*Ghassalt idék?*' (Did you wash your hands?), Papa would ask me. When in doubt, he ordered me to let him smell my palm. If it was perfumed, he nodded his head with a satisfied look; if not, he unceremoniously sent me back to the bathroom. At the table, no mischief, no capriciousness, no dropped forks, no spilled glasses of water. Moreover, we had to wait until we were seven years old to have the honour of leaving the kitchen to sit at our father's table. Each of us had an assigned seat, always the same. My father sat to the right of my mother, who had the seat of honour – proof of the great respect he had for her. And I sat to the right of my father. He brought his interns' gems home to us and the incidents that took place at the court-house, such as this retort from a courageous witness: 'If I dare say so, Your Honour, it's that, like you, I don't have faith in justice!' or that of a judge addressing an elderly woman who claimed to be only forty years old: 'With all due respect, Ma'am, from which age do you begin counting?' The anecdotes he humorously told us were always magnified, exaggerated, 'sprinkled with salt and pepper' as a well-known Lebanese expression says: thanks to his verve, the most banal event was transformed into a veritable odyssey!

During every meal, my father monopolized the conversation, so much so that he was always the last to finish his plate. He had his favourite dishes: he liked *tabouleh*, *foul* (broad beans in oil), *baténjén mé'lé* (slices of fried aubergine), fish, but he didn't care for either pizza or hamburgers. He had a great passion for fruit: bananas (which he called '*mozé*' rather than '*maouzé*', with the southern Lebanese accent), grapes, apples, plums, peaches, pears, as long as they were from the garden. When he ate figs, he had the strange habit of peeling them with a knife, cutting them in half, then taking off his glasses in order to inspect their insides for fear they might be infested with worms. He had an innermost conviction that all fruit was beneficial to our health, and exhorted us to consume it abundantly. If he sensed we were reticent, he would place a piece of fruit on our plate and declare in an authoritarian tone, '*Mnél jnainé*!', a conclusive argument we were not allowed to oppose.

In the afternoon, we would play in the garden while he took a nap. Beware he who made too much of a commotion! Upon awakening, the Admiral would make his rounds in the house to inspect our activities. Only board games found favour in his eyes. Marbles and toy soldiers, deemed to be childish and mindless, were strictly forbidden. His nightmare? An indoor game of English origin called Subbuteo, a miniature version of a football game, which consisted of flicking tiny figurines on a big green cloth in the shape of a football field that had to be spread out on a rug.

The objective of the game was, as in real football games, to get the little white ball into the opponent's goal. On all fours or sprawled out on the ground, we played endless games and positioned a lookout in the living room to warn us – by coughing – of Father's imminent arrival. As soon as the alarm was given and my father's resolute footsteps echoed in the antechamber, we would panic: we would roll up the cloth with the game-pieces and the ball, hide it under the bed and pretend to be talking to one another or looking through a book. A dangerous exercise that we successfully completed in under six seconds, the time it took him to cross the hallway and burst into our bedroom. Once he caught us. His hands on his hips, he gave us a look that revealed his disappointment, then he shook his head and, without a word, turned on his heels. It was probably difficult for someone who spent his life with a pen in his hand, buried in books and files, to conceive that his children could be engrossed in useless distractions. How could we hold it against him? We did not revolt, did not criticize – even amongst ourselves – this state of affairs, but we took advantage of his daily nap to go against the set rules and to devote ourselves to games for which he did not care.

In the evening, we would watch television until eight thirty. Then it was time for prayers. In May, in celebration of the month of Mary, we sang canticles, gathered around a candle provided by Mama and a photograph of the Virgin of Harissa, an amazing photograph of the statue on its pedestal with the moon serving as her halo, for which my father had a fondness. With his beautiful voice, the Admiral recited *Ave Maria*, *L'ombre s'étend sur la terre*, *Ya oumm Allah* and, standing side by side, we sang the choruses. In conclusion, he recited *Our Father*, using formal references to God: '*Thy* will be done.' When he closed his eyes to pray better, we would hit one another and make faces; as soon as he opened them again, we would be well-behaved. After this ceremonial, lights-out was declared. Sleep thus became obligatory, whether or not we were tired. Not a word, not a whisper was permitted. A half-hour after our lights were turned off, my father would perform raids, unannounced visits to our rooms, in order to verify that everything was in order and that we were in fact in bed. If he had a doubt, he would turn on a flashlight and search our faces for the blink of an eyelid or a grin. In spite of his thorough inspections, we always found a way, as soon as he had turned his back, to talk in low voices, to have a pillow fight or to tiptoe to the kitchen and bring back *markouk*[1] bread, which we ate under the covers: in the morning, the beds were strewn with crumbs. As for me, when Morpheus was slow in taking me in his arms, I would choose a book and lock myself in the bathroom to read at more leisure, sitting on the toilet seat. If my father knocked on the door, I would tell him, affecting a sleepy voice: 'My stomach hurts, Father. I'll be out in five minutes.'

---

1. Paper-thin rounds of bread.

'Hurry up!' he would respond, sternly.

Henry Miller was the author of a surprising essay entitled 'Reading in the Toilet', in which he evokes the act of reading in this intimate location. Had he known me, he no doubt would have told the story of how, thanks to my father, I acquired a passion for reading in the toilet ...

Crime and Punishment

My father enjoyed hiking. Every Sunday, wearing his cap and his hiking boots, armed with his alpenstock, he would take off across fields, valleys and mountains to get some fresh air and admire nature. I only have to close my eyes and I can see the Holy Valley again, the Qadicha, in the northern part of the country, with its monasteries clinging to the rocks, ancient refuges for persecuted Christians, its caves decorated with frescoes, its terraced gardens, its majestic trees, and the translucent fog that rises like incense at day's end. The Knight of Arvieux who, in the seventeenth century, sojourned for an extended period in the Levant, was rendered speechless at the sight of this landscape: 'When one looks out at the valley platform where the cedars are, the mountains alongside it form the most pleasant and diversified perspective in the world [...],' he wrote in his Memoirs. 'We went to the end of the valley of the saints, from whence we saw an infinite number of caves which had been the dwellings of these anchorite saints. What puzzled us was how they could have reached them to live there. They are so high above the valley floor, and carved into such steep precipices that they appear to be inaccessible on all sides; it seems they could only be suitable for birds and that one would need wings to reach them. After giving it great thought, we decided they must have climbed down to them from the least impassible spots, with ladders or ropes.' Every summer, I accompanied my father to this sacred place: he knew its paths, shortcuts, springs and convents as well as the shepherd with the curved moustache who played his *nay* – that reed flute with sad tones – for us while watching over his flock. At the end of our journey, we would go to pay our respects to the Maronite Patriarch in his summer residence in Dimane, a haven of peace and prayer. With deference, my father would place his right hand over his heart, bow, and kiss the holy man's ring. I would imitate him, blushing as I did so.

Occasionally we would climb down to the Jeita cave, a natural cathedral sculpted by the alchemy of time and water. Making my way through stalactites and stalagmites, I had the strange impression that I was entering the mouth of a sleeping whale, but fortunately this sensation was tempered by the beauty of the concretions with their changing colours and by the bracing coolness of the place. Twice a month we would walk as far as Faraya, known for its ski resort and its inhabitants' legendary laziness. 'A guy from Faraya is hitchhiking. A car drives past, brakes ten yards ahead and waits for him. The guy doesn't move. Cupping his hands around his mouth, he yells to the driver: "Thanks man, but you stopped where I wanted to be dropped off!'" My father told me this joke often. I would smile as if I were hearing it for the first time, thinking that his extraordinary vitality made him the exact opposite of the poor old hitchhiker. If it was not too hot out, we would continue on to Faqra. This site, which Ernest Renan considered to be 'the mountain's most spectacular group of ruins', intrigued my father, who did not understand the reasons which had driven the Romans to build those merlon-capped cubic structures and that temple – dedicated to the 'very great god' – there, in the middle of nowhere. 'How the devil did they move these stone blocks? Who dreamed up this insane project?' he wondered, his perplexity comparable to that of the Knight of Arvieux before the Holy Valley's monastic cells. His hands crossed on the knob of his walking stick, the Admiral contemplated these relics with the eyes of a child.

One morning, we stopped in front of a monastery that was under construction, perched on a high hill overhanging the Mediterranean. From there, the view was breathtaking: Jounieh Bay was there before us, a perfect arc of a circle clasped around a turquoise sea. A monk was sitting on a bench, exhausted. He informed my father that he had begun to build a monastery with his own money, but that he did not have sufficient funds to see his project through to the end. He was in such despair, and the surrounding landscape was so enchanting, that my father did not hesitate: he bought the monastery. But the war came, which prevented him from taking advantage of this acquisition: the militia installed a field gun and transformed the crypt into a blockhouse.

From his many hikes, my father always brought back sticks, which he carefully stored behind the radiator in his bedroom in case he needed to punish us. For in order to control his six children, strictness was necessary. But it was not blind: the punishments inflicted by my father were reserved for scoundrels and dunces. They were of two categories: the stick and kneeling. The first form of punishment reprimanded bad behaviour. It was administered to the culprit's backside with a reddish stick, which was at once hard and flexible like a whip, and was poetically named *adib al-roummane*: the branch of the pomegranate tree. An Arabic proverb says, '*Al-aassa li man aassa*': The stick for rebels. My father applied it literally.

The other form of punishment, much less painful, consisted of kneeling for an hour to atone for our crimes. We were subjected to this form individually or collectively, as the result of a wide variety of offences: for instance, when Leonardo practised his artistic talents on the living room walls, when we had rock fights with our neighbours, or when the second set of twins locked themselves in the bathroom and turned on all the taps at once, causing a flood upstairs. Lyautey was a regular of this punishment: my father would order him to kneel in his room for the entire duration of his nap. The sound of our laughter, carrying up from the garden, merely increased our little brother's suffering. He would thus contrive to make all sorts of little noises to hasten the awakening of the Admiral, which was synonymous with release. Once liberated, he would tear down the stairs and join our horde with the frenzy of a drug addict going through withdrawal.

One day, we were all subjected to the dreaded punishment together. I recall the scene perfectly:

'*Ya chabéb*,[1] come on!'

Upon returning home from school, I notice the sprinklers that a technician has just installed in the four corners of the garden to water the lawn. I have hardly spoken the words when my brothers, my sister and my three cousins gather around me. Our eyes filled with wonder, we admire the sprays of water that are spouting from the stakes driven into the ground. The temptation is too great. Without thinking, we dash forward, and, with our arms in the air, leap about on the lawn, letting out shrieks of joy that end up disturbing my father's nap. Irritated, he gets up, opens the shutters of his first-floor bedroom, and to his astonishment, sees nine scoundrels doing somersaults among the sprinklers, which, with a regular motion, are spraying them generously.

'All of you, take off your shoes and get up here!'

My father's voice rings out so loudly it echoes off Mount Sannine in the distance. Our blood runs cold. We look at

---

1. 'Guys' in Arabic.

one another, distraught, at once disappointed at having to bring our aquatic games to an end and terrorized at the idea of having to bear the wrath of the Admiral.

'All of us?' I ask, pointing at my three cousins, in the hope that they be spared my father's anger.

'All of you!'

We obey. Barefoot, soaked to the bone, we climb the staircase that separates us from his bedroom. My father is sitting at his desk, writing assiduously. Without raising his eyes from his work, he mumbles: 'All nine of you, kneel down on the rug in front of me. Nobody is to move!'

No one revolts. We kneel down and remain there, side by side, dripping wet, backs straight, lips tensed. As for the Admiral, he continues to write as if nothing were out of the ordinary, and does not even deign to look at us. Finally, an hour later, he signals to us that we can leave by brushing us away with a wave of his hand. We get up without a word, rub our knees, which have gone numb, and take our leave, certain we have received a fair punishment for our crime. Suddenly, my father calls me back. I turn around. With his index finger, he signals for me to approach him. I obey.

'I'm disappointed,' he tells me dryly. 'The eldest should always set a good example.'

I hang my head and leave his room. I feel like I have the weight of Mount Sannine on my frail shoulders.

Habits

My father had tics and habits. Who doesn't? He always washed his hands thoroughly, making the soap lather (this movement produced a suction cup sound), then rubbed them with alcohol to 'kill the germs'; took a nap every afternoon with a black satin mask over his eyes; bound his files with a thin hemp cord; never wrote a contract containing thirteen clauses, so as not to bring the client bad luck; used yellowed rough-paper; placed a pillow on the seat of his chair in order to be comfortable while writing; kept a silk handkerchief in his pocket in spite of the fact that this was a long-lost practice; never went walking on a Sunday without his hat even when the skies were grey; and turned out the lights in empty rooms to save electricity or turned them on if we were reading in the dark, reproaching us for 'ruining' our eyes. He collected rosaries, not the kind used for praying, but the *massabéh* that one rubs to pass the time; he bought four newspapers every day – two in Arabic (*An-Nahar* and

Al-Amal) and two in French (*L'Orient Le Jour* and *Le Réveil*) – and every Friday he bought two weekly French-language magazines (*La Revue du Liban* and *Magazine*). He did not like to see newspapers lying around on the armchairs and made us wash our hands after looking through them because of the black ink that stained our fingertips. He read them from cover to cover, lingering over the obituaries (he never missed going to offer his condolences, conscious of the importance placed on this social obligation in the Orient), and did not overlook a single piece of news, to the point that he was capable of accurately naming all the players on the French football team or any given princess's groom-cum-lover ... He never threw them away, under the pretext that he might need them for work some day, with the result that our attic became a veritable dumping ground with mounds of newspapers piled higgledy-piggledy amongst broken toys. It took the war and the destruction of our house for my father to finally resign himself to giving up his dusty archives.

The Admiral also had his sartorial habits: custom tailored suits, monogrammed dress shirts, cuff links, Derek & Rose pyjamas, lisle socks ... He was fond of ties, wore them all the time and knotted them with such skill that we were always asking him to help us with ours: he would obediently comply, pleased to demonstrate his know-how. He always wore the same cologne, 4711, an ancient fragrance that could count among its illustrious clients Napoleon himself. According to Father, the Emperor placed such importance on fragrances that while exiled on the island of Saint Helena he asked that two blocks of Houbigant's tuberose be burned in an incense dish upon his death ...

My father did not care for manual work. I never saw him tinker, cook, do the dishes, repair a toy or a bicycle chain, type ... How would he have survived had he lived alone after the death of his mother? He was fascinated by technology ('Ah, those Japanese!' he often said in amazement), but made no effort to master it: turning on the VCR, handling a camera or video camera, using a computer ... all of these things were beyond him. But though he was not good with his hands, he liked to shave and went about his daily shaving ritual with such concentration that he was furious at having to interrupt it when anxious clients called early in the morning with questions. I recall the scene perfectly. Above the sink, my father sets out his tools: a dishevelled shaving brush, an ageless razor, fearsome blades bearing the name Wilkinson Sword and adorned with two crossed sabres, a tube of shaving cream, a small plastic bowl. He lathers the shaving soap in the bowl with his shaving brush, then inserts a blade removed from a small white wrapper into the razor. And the ritual begins. His movements are slow and short. The shaving is done in the direction the hair grows: from top to bottom on his cheeks, above his lips and on his chin; from front to back under his chin; from the bottom up on his neck. After half an hour, he sets down his razor, gazes at himself in the mirror, rinses his face, wipes it with a large blue towel, then sprays himself with cologne. His face tightens from the burning sensation: as he does every morning, he has cut his chin or his neck. He curses and blots at the cut with a towel. He is bleeding, but too bad. There isn't time: the hearing at the court-house is at eight o'clock. There is a small bloodstain on the collar of the white shirt he wears, the implacable signature of the Wilkinson Sword.

As a child, I marvelled at this spectacle, regretting the fact that I was still beardless. I believed this deprived me of a great happiness, and had no idea this undertaking was, for all men, a real chore that robbed them of precious minutes of sleep. For all men but my father! For shaving was never a chore in his eyes. He took advantage of this rare moment, when he was holding something other than a pen in his hand and concentrating on something other than a file, to clear his head and to ... sing. Yes, my father liked to sing while shaving. He had a beautiful voice and sang in tune. He said he had his mother's gift, a saintly woman named Minerve. What did he sing? Four songs, always the same, gleaned from the repertoire of his past:

> *Padam ... Padam ... Padam ...*
> *Il arrive en courant derrière moi*
> *Padam ... Padam ... Padam ...*
> *Il me fait le coup du souviens-toi.*

> *Padam ... Padam ... Padam ...*
> *He runs up to me, so tender*
> *Padam ... Padam ... Padam ...*
> *And pulls the old 'do you remember?'*

For a long time this verse intrigued me. What did *'Padam'* mean? And why was the man running after the young woman? Still today I admit that I do not understand the true meaning of these lyrics by Edith Piaf, his favourite singer along with Tino Rossi, who sang the following verse:

> *Voulez-vous danser, grand-mère*
> *Voulez-vous valser, grand-père*
> *Tout comme au bon vieux temps*
> *Quand vous aviez vingt ans*
> *Sur un air qui vous rappelle*
> *Combien la vie était belle.*

> Would you like to dance, grandmother
> Would you like to dance, grandfather
> Just like the good old days
> When you were young and gay
> To a song that recalls
> How lovely life was.

This refrain moved my father deeply; the reason escaped me at the time, but I am no longer in the dark: his maternal grandfather had collapsed before his eyes after having a heart attack while dancing to this song. My father probably continued to sing it in tribute to this ancestor whose fragile heart had not been able to withstand a dance.

The other two songs did not have any words. Or so I thought. I heard my father hum the melodies ('Tana naniana naniana ...'), unable to identify their origin. It was by chance, during two concerts, that I was able to assign titles to them. The first melody revealed itself to me during a recital given by Luciano Pavarotti at the Beirut Sports City. Suddenly, before the admiring eyes of thousands of spectators, with his powerful voice, he broke into a traditional song entitled '*Mamma*', during which I recognized, with great emotion, the old melody I had heard each morning during my father's shaving ritual:

> *Mamma, son tanto felice*
> *Perché ritorno da te*
> *La mia canzone ti dice*
> *Ch'e il più bel giorno per me*
> *Mamma, son tanto felice*
> *Viver lontanto perché? ...*

My father did not speak Italian. But he had always been so devoted to his mother that his song choice could not have been fortuitous. Was it out of modesty that he didn't sing the lyrics?

The other melody revealed its secret to me a few months later, during a recital given by another Italian artist, Andrea Bocelli. At the Beiteddine Festival, in the courtyard of a magnificent eighteenth-century Ottoman palace, beneath a moon so low it appeared to be drawing near to better hear the music, the blind singer walked on stage on the arm of the conductor and, his back straight, with a faraway look in his eyes, began the first song of his repertoire, written for Enrico Caruso by Salvatore Cardillo:

> *Catarí, Catarí,*
> *Pecchè me dici sti parole amare?*

> Catarí, Catarí,
> Why do you have such bitter words for me?

I jumped: so the mysterious melody that came from my father's lips every morning was '*Catarí*'! I closed my eyes to savour the lyrics which, as if by magic, grafted themselves onto the familiar tune my father used to hum! I had come full circle. I *knew* now. No part of my father's early morning songs remained a mystery any longer. What did they have in common? Love – for lover, mother, grandmother – but also tenderness and nostalgia ... So my father was a romantic. His songs had given him away.

Going Out

My father did not like us to go out. Before the age of eighteen, we were not allowed to go dancing or to go out in the evening. Once we were eighteen, if we went to a party, he would patiently await our return and, sitting in the hallway, would not sleep a wink until we got home. Dance clubs were unknown to him. Moreover, he hated modern music, which he invariably called pop music, and always asked us to turn down the radio when we were listening to rock or disco songs. In the sixties, when Johnny Hallyday was turned away at Beirut airport by order of the Minister of the Interior, who judged him to be harmful to young people, I don't imagine my father found the initiative to be uncalled-for.

The Admiral cared even less for travelling: he considered aeroplanes to be dangerous and preferred to have us by his side. My mother, who dreamed of going to Italy with him, secretly regretted this. One day, for their thirtieth wedding anniversary, we insisted that he sign a declaration promising to take her to Venice at the first opportunity. First he protested, but in the end affixed his signature to the bottom of the document.

Shortly thereafter, he had to bring himself to part with us: the Liberation War launched by General Aoun against the Syrians in 1989 was raging; the schools and universities had closed their doors. What were we to do? Faithful to his principles, he did not for a single moment consider packing his things and leaving, but resigned himself to sending all six of us to France to continue our studies. That was a dreadful year for him. Accustomed to being surrounded by his tribe, he suddenly found himself deprived of our laughter and mischief, condemned to dining alone with my mother in a deserted house. To fill his solitude, I wrote him letters in which I reassured him by sending news of his children who 'are studying hard, eating healthy food and going to bed early'. One evening, I even wrote him a sort of prose poem of which I kept a copy:

> *All these months that separate me from you make my life hell. If I had only one message for you, it would be that oblivion will not take anything away and that I love you. Sometimes, I wonder what you are doing at the moment I am thinking of you, and I tell myself that all those gestures I do not see, and yet that I know by heart, are unjustly eluding me. Sometimes I also tell myself how stupid I was to hurt you, and I will never forgive myself.*
>
> *My solitude here is becoming barren. I will be with*

you again soon. When one has tasted absence, the moment of reunion has another flavour: in the kisses that are exchanged there is also the violent desire to never part again, the intense will to make up for the lost hours and to control time, for ever.

Absence is precious: without it, we would never know whether or not we love someone merely out of habit. From the moment it forces us to break with our habits, that comfortable ossification, it is as if our feelings had been dusted off.

When all's said and done, I do not regret anything. Neither the tears shed, nor these past months without you … For I have become a man and I have acquired this indomitable certainty: that you are everything for me and that I adore you!

My father never answered my letter. But when I returned from France, he called me into his room. He showed me the poem, carefully framed and placed on the dresser near his bed. Drawing close, he hugged me to his heart and held me for a long moment. Behind his glasses, there were tears.

Mr Samir

As a child, I did not dare admit to my father that I liked literature for fear of disappointing him: though he was cultivated, he feared this consuming passion would cause me to abandon my pursuit of a career in law. I owe this love to the war. Deprived of school by the bombings, hidden away in the neighbourhood shelter, I only had one distraction: reading. My mother, I admit, encouraged me a great deal, took advantage of cease-fires to buy new books for me and gave me things like *The Diary of Anne Frank* to read, which I still remember fondly. As for my youngest brothers, they preferred to take advantage of those idle moments to learn a foreign language. While Leonardo had no trouble getting hold of *Italian in 90 Lessons*, Le Corbusier found himself condemned to learning the language of Goethe with the help of a Philips vacuum cleaner owner's manual which was written in German and French. When asked '*Sprechen Sie Deutsch?*' (Do you speak German?), he invariably responded with the first sentence from the manual: '*Drücken Sie die START-Taste*' (Push the Start button).

Around the age of nine, I wrote a novel that was about thirty pages long, entitled 'Bob on a Cruise' and subtitled 'Reckless Bob's Adventure', which my mother laboriously typed and which Leonardo took pleasure in illustrating. Although the book bore the following awkward dedication: 'For my dear father, with all my affection and my great admiration,' I did not have the courage to show it to the Admiral. I can still see myself, sitting before my typescript, perplexed, torn between the desire to submit it to him in the hope that I might evoke a smile of encouragement, and the fear of seeing him shake his head in dismay before what he probably considered to be 'a waste of time'. Prompted by the ambition to make my book known as soon as possible and to imitate the precocious Minou Drouet, who had published her poems at the age of seven and a half, I made the decision to contact a publisher without the help of my parents. How was I to proceed? At school, I had read with great interest a book entitled *Two Years' Vacation*, reprinted by a local publisher, Samir Booksellers. I naively believed that my book was in the same vein as Jules Verne's novel and could thus legitimately appear in the same collection. So I looked through the phone book for the number of the publisher in question and, taking advantage of my father's nap, sat down in the dining room and called them. A man's voice answered.

'Mr Samir, please,' I said, taking on a deep voice.

'Speaking.'

My heart skipped a beat. How was I to begin the conversation, how was I to mention my project without making a fool of myself? I took my courage in both hands.

'Good afternoon, sir. I'm a young author and I would like to submit the manuscript of my first novel entitled 'Bob on a Cruise', the story of a guy who frees some prisoners being held hostage on an island ...'

My proposal was met with silence. And then: 'How old are you, son?'

How was I to respond? My childlike voice had given me away.

'Um ... fifteen, I'm fifteen years old,' I lied.

'Let me speak to your father!'

My father! How on earth could I let him speak to my father who knew nothing about this? And how could I explain my initiative to the Admiral without arousing his disapproval? Finding myself in an awkward position, I beat a retreat and abruptly hung up.

When night came, I burst into tears, burying my head in my pillow. Alerted by my sobs, my mother came running in to see me.

'What's wrong, ya *albé*?'[1] my mother asked, stroking my hair.

I wiped away my tears and looked at her despairingly: 'I'll never be like Minou Drouet!'

---

1. A term of endearment that means 'sweetheart' in Arabic.

Censorship

Every evening at eight o'clock, my father watched the news. To do so he crouched down, a strange position that evidently helped him relax, and, like a yogi, he remained motionless throughout the broadcast. We gathered around him, sitting cross-legged on the rug, not always understanding what the announcer reeled off in Arabic. The other show he never missed was the one with an old man wearing a nightcap ('He was my Arabic teacher in the Jesuit school') who spoke about the history of Lebanon. Erudite though he was, the man eventually grew tiresome. He made frequent digressions and, for an hour and a half, nothing livened up his monologue. Father did not oblige us to watch this programme, thank God, but he highly recommended it, 'to enrich our cultural knowledge', he would say. Our only goal being to please him and to be forgiven for having misbehaved, we occasionally forced ourselves to watch the show without understanding any of the learned man's words, taking great care to arrive late to shorten our suffering.

My father liked Sacha Guitry. He would often repeat his witticisms and never missed an opportunity to tell this anecdote: one day, while Guitry is getting a shave in his library, one of his friends bursts into his house and begs him to lend him one of his books. He is met with a refusal. Cut to the quick, he vehemently protests: 'To me, your friend, you refuse to lend a book!' And Guitry retorts: 'You see all these books? They belong to friends!' The moral of the story, my father would say, is that books are too precious to lend ...

He also liked Harry Baur whom he took to be the greatest actor of all time, and whose tragic end he bitterly regretted: Baur had been arrested and tortured by the Gestapo in 1942 because he was suspected of being Jewish. Released by the Nazis, he never overcame his suffering and died at home in April 1943. 'You should have seen him play Rasputin, Jean Valjean or Tarass Boulba!' my father would say to us with childlike exuberance. 'That actor could do anything!' I admit to having been slightly disappointed upon watching one of Harry Baur's films, entitled *L'Assassinat du Père Noël* (Who Killed Santa Claus?): it seemed to me that Father's judgment was somewhat exaggerated. Moreover, his film choices were paradoxical: he liked Fernandel, especially in the role of Don Camillo (the larger-than-life priest who confronts Peppone, the communist mayor of his village), but not Louis de Funès whom he considered to be 'affected', while in fact one is just as much so as the other; he liked Chouchou, a Lebanese actor, but not Abou Salim whom he considered to be too 'vulgar', although both were popular actors. He had blacklisted all Lebanese and Egyptian films, which he thought insipid, but encouraged us to watch a local series entitled *Abou Melhem*, which was as sanctimonious as could be. Our surprise reached new heights one day: while we were watching an action film on television with the duo Bud Spencer and Terence Hill, masters of the art of fist-fighting, he crouched down next to us and began to watch, laughing heartily. We were dumbfounded: we had never imagined our father could be amused by those two actors, for whom the film critics had such contempt!

Our father's tastes became our own. With a few exceptions: defying his orders, I often watched Egyptian films on television, thanks to the complicity of our Syrian nanny whose name was Shakwa, literally 'Complaint' (the ultimate for a lawyer), who, when my parents went out to dinner, would let me watch them with her. Najla' Fathi, Faten Hamama, Hussein Fehmi, Mahmoud Yassine, Rushdy Abaza ... I learned to recognize the great Egyptian actors and, little did my parents know, became an expert on Arabic films.

As the eldest child, my father entrusted me with the task of previewing video cassettes before allowing my siblings to watch them. Taking my role as censor very seriously, I would shut myself away in the small living room and watch the films my mother had chosen at the neighbourhood video store. If there was too much kissing or there were nude scenes, I was to blacklist the film. If not, the video received my stamp of approval. Considering these criteria, only westerns and animated films were spared censorship!

In reality, it wasn't until the age of thirty that I had the opportunity to go to see a film with my father. Accompanying us to the cinema was a task reserved for my mother, who never missed a chance to take us to the Embassy cinema where the Walt Disney, Charlie Chaplin and Laurel and Hardy or *Les Charlots*[1] films were shown. Too engrossed in his work, my father granted himself little leisure time, be it for his own activities or for ours, and I do not think we would have had the opportunity to enjoy his presence among us had not the war, paralysing the courts, forced him to stay home for long months. One day, Father came looking for me: 'Let's go to see a film,' he said.

'Excuse me?' I said, dumbfounded.

'They're showing *Titanic* at the Empire cinema. I invited both my brothers and I thought you might like to come along with us!'

I could not help but smile. At the age of thirty, I would finally experience the pleasure of seeing a film with him! But a sudden doubt crossed my mind: during a lecture he gave in Beirut, the writer François Nourissier had told the story of how his father had died by his side in a cinema. He had

---

1. A troupe of French comedy actors who were popular in the 1970s.

suddenly fallen asleep, never to awaken again. Was there a chance the Admiral, who was not as young as he used to be, would meet the same end?

The following day, we went as planned to the Empire cinema and met my two uncles in the lobby. They had not been to a film in thirty years either.

'The last film I saw was *Casablanca*,' the first one said.

'It was *Spartacus* for me,' the second one declared nostalgically. 'I saw it at the Martyrs' Square before it was destroyed.'

We bought popcorn and sat in the middle row. While on the screen the ship's passengers were struggling against the billows, I began to contemplate my father's profile, his slightly hooked nose, his large forehead, his myopic eyes that were glued to the screen. He was at once uncomfortable in his seat – he had lost the habit of being confined in a cinema for two to three hours – and very impressed by the images unfolding before him: on his face, I saw what was probably the same expression of surprise and concern that could be found on the faces of the spectators of the first Lumière brothers' film ... I took his hand and squeezed it tightly to keep him from falling asleep as François Nourissier's father had. He smiled at me. At the end of the film, I saw people, deeply moved, crying out of sadness. Mine were tears of joy.

Film Club

'*Yalla ya chabéb*, get up!'

That night, I wake my brothers and my sister after carefully verifying that Father has gone to bed. In our pyjamas, all six of us go down the stairs leading to the dining room and, in the dark, sit down in front of the television. I pull the video cassette out of its case and, with an expert hand, put it into the VCR which starts playing. Soon after, the title of the film appears on the screen: *Texas Chainsaw Massacre*. We hold our breath. Bissé squeezes my hand, Fred Astaire bites his lips. The morbid atmosphere of the film is accentuated by the surrounding darkness and the bluish light given off by the television. The sense of guilt that grips us is not as strong as our curiosity: we like horror films and the strong emotions they evoke.

Suddenly, around midnight, we hear footsteps. We look at one another, paralysed with fear. Those are Father's slippers. In one bound, I rush to the television and turn it off. The sound grows nearer. The Admiral is coming down the stairs. We count twenty-two steps. We are overcome with anxiety: we're done for. What will he say? What will become of us? I suddenly feel responsible for having got my siblings involved in this mess. I cannot even imagine the miserable moment that likely awaits us. But we have to do something! Instinctively, we all hide together under the dining room table and huddle up against one another. The slippers are now only a few yards from us. My father enters the room and walks across it to get to the kitchen. He opens the refrigerator and takes out a bottle of water. We hear him take a glass, fill it, and take a drink. We hold our breath, trembling like the victims in the film we have just interrupted. Papa comes back through the living room, walks up the stairs, and goes back into his bedroom. We remain motionless for at least fifteen minutes, just to collect our wits. One by one, we finally climb out of our hiding place.

'Should we watch the rest of the film?' Lyautey asks me.

'*Majnoun*? Are you crazy?'

I give him a friendly tap on the back of the neck and motion for him to go to bed. In single file, we go back to our bedrooms, at once disappointed at having ended our film night and relieved at not having been caught red-handed.

The following morning at breakfast, Mama is surprised to see us looking so poorly.

'It's normal,' observes the Admiral, peeling a fig. 'If they slept instead of clowning around they'd be in great shape!'

Childhood Long Ago

I know nothing, or very little, about the Admiral's childhood, his adolescence, the period before he was married. Does it matter? What I care about, after all, is having known him since I came into the world, since he became my father. And yet, more than once I have wanted to ask him about it, to invite him to tell me about his past, to share his memories with me. Each time, I changed my mind: he was so busy that for him to sacrifice two hours of his time to tell me about his life would have been unthinkable. And had he agreed to go along with this game, would he have told me the whole truth? Who can claim to know everything about a person? Is it ever possible to uncover all of someone's secrets, however close they are? As wrinkles formed on his broad forehead, as his hair greyed, I increasingly regretted not being able to save the stories his prodigious memory had stored up, like an ornithologist who records the song of an endangered species.

All I know about my father's childhood is that he was a studious boy. I have a picture of him in which he is reading while eating, proof that, even very early, he did not waste time. He began his schooling in the south, in Saida with the Marist Brothers (at the time, his parents lived in a traditional Lebanese house, which is still standing, a stone's throw from the sea), and continued it in Beirut with the Jesuits at Saint Joseph University. There was a seminarian there who played a significant role in his life. His name was Tresca. He thought highly of my father, entrusted him with heavy responsibilities and believed in him. Upon learning of his death, burned to death in his tank at the gates of Damascus during the fratricidal war that, in 1941, brought Gaullists and Vichyites into conflict, Father was overwhelmed with an unspeakable sadness. More than sixty years later, he would recall the memory of his mentor with this same sadness.

My father had a very special relationship with his sister: he protected her, kept close track of her when she went out, and, at night, patiently awaited her return before going to bed. 'For me, he was the symbol of work and duty,' she recalls. 'He radiated such force that his presence alone reassured us.' On Christmas Eve, they sang duets for the entire family, 'Adeste Fideles' and 'Mary, Our Lady', accompanied by their elder brother who played the piano. There was a very strong bond between my father and this brother. Though they had very different personalities, they were thick as thieves. One day, for a fancy-dress party organized by a certain Mr

Kemp, the eldest decided to dress up as Harpo, one of the Marx Brothers, and set out in search of red check trousers to complete his outfit. Having scoured all the shops in Beirut to no avail, he asked Father for advice, who remembered having seen a neighbour wearing a pair of trousers matching that description. Without a moment's hesitation, the two brothers went to the man's house, and he just happened to be wearing the coveted item of clothing that day. Embarrassed, they explained the purpose of their visit to him. The kind man disappeared behind a screen, pulled off his trousers and, looking amused, gave them to the two boys. My uncle thanked him and hurried home to change. At the fancy-dress party, the red check trousers were a big hit. 'Where on earth did he dig those up?' the guests wondered. Dressed as Richelieu, my father was careful not to reveal the secret.

My father also got along wonderfully with his two other brothers, although they had left the country, one for Africa, the other for America. In spite of this separation, they remained very close, forever bound together by fraternal solidarity.

What kind of relationship did he have with his own father? I know my grandfather was a lawyer, that he had studied at the time of the Ottoman Empire, perhaps in Constantinople, and that he was so irritable he had the unfortunate habit of breaking his umbrella over the heads of annoying individuals.

'Don't be irritable like me if you want to succeed in this profession,' he had warned my father, who followed his advice and overcame his short temper. There is still an old man at the court-house who has worked with three generations of lawyers and knew my grandfather. When I see him, I tell myself that he is the last witness, the final survivor of a bygone era ... My grandfather was not a practising Catholic. Upset by this, my father took him to church one day and asked him to go to confession. Ten minutes later, my grandfather came out of the confessional, visibly infuriated.

'So, did everything go OK?' my father asked him, worried.

'That crazy damned priest ordered me to recite the act of contrition twenty times! Twenty times – can you imagine?'

Offended by my grandfather's vulgar language, the Admiral took him by the elbow and asked him to go back into the confessional.

Mine

My mother and father had a unique relationship: they never argued. No inappropriate remarks, no squabbling over trifles. Was it thanks to my mother's good nature? Was it because of their age difference – seventeen years! – which made their relations more mature, more serene? I could not say. All I know is they got along wonderfully, so well that for a long time I thought all couples were the same. They called one another 'Mine'; every morning they had coffee together, just the two of them, and confided in one another. How did they meet? At the age of forty-three, my father still lived with his mother and did not think he would marry. Realizing she was fighting a losing battle, my grandmother used emotional blackmail on him, which ended up being very effective: 'If you don't marry, I'll die an unhappy woman. Do you want me to go out with a heavy heart?' He immediately set out in search of that someone special. And he found her leaving church: with her gentle manner, her diaphanous skin, her expressive eyes, my mother was attractive to him in every way. He fell under her spell and began to regularly attend the ten o'clock mass to contemplate her from a distance. My father always objected to this version: 'I went to pray,' he maintained, unable to admit that someone as serious as himself could be weak enough to go to church out of love. After a short engagement, they were married. At the end of the ceremony, when it was time to sign the marriage certificate, the Admiral did something that made the guests laugh: rather than mechanically signing the document, he had a very lawyer-like reaction: he put on his reading glasses and leaned over the certificate to read it carefully and verify its contents before affixing his signature to it.

In spite of his work, my father was touchingly attentive to my mother. When he travelled, he had a knack for buying dresses that looked beautiful on her. 'I spot a saleslady in the shop who is about your size and I ask her to try it on for me,' my father would explain. 'If it fits her, that means it will fit you.' He would gently tease her about her cooking, claiming that during the first six months of their marriage they ate nothing but scallops – the only dish she knew how to prepare at the time – and also about her passion for gardening. One day, for her birthday, with an ironic look in his eye, he gave her the perfect gardener's outfit – a pair of denim overalls, clippers, a shovel, a spade and a watering can. He sometimes called her Madame de Sévigné because of the innumerable letters she wrote to her sister, who had settled in Grenoble, and to a married couple she knew in Lyons.

During the war, my parents never left each other's side. While the fighting was raging and the Syrian army was bombarding Beirut, they stayed together in spite of everything. Even when, overcome with fear, all six of us decided to take refuge in the country house of some friends, then to leave for France, my mother refused to follow us so she could stay by 'Mine's' side. Once peace had returned, he wrote her this touching letter, as if, assessing the scale of the sacrifices she had made, he suddenly felt the need to pay tribute to her:

My darling,

I offer you these few words as a token of my love and admiration. I think of you with a paroxysm of affection. Today, more than ever, I feel the immense happiness with which you have filled our household, thanks to your unwavering faith, your tenderness, your unswerving devotion, your ethereal serenity and your ever-welcoming smile.

In the midst of the upheaval that has shaken our country and the tragic events we have been through, you have shown sublime courage and remarkable calm, which I imagine concealed your anguish, but which allowed us to overcome those ordeals together. Our faith in God and the ardour of our love elevated us to a higher ground.

Signed 'Devotedly yours', this carefully written letter reassured me in my conviction that beneath his armour of severity there lay a tender heart.

One day, I asked my mother: 'Mama, if you had to choose between Father and the six of us, whom would you choose?' This incongruous question seemed to make her uncomfortable. Why choose? After a moment's hesitation, she answered in a solemn voice: 'Mine.'

Assistants

My father did not know how to drive, in spite of the fact that by some miracle he had managed to obtain a driving licence. The one time he decided to give it another try, he came back on foot with the gear lever in his hand: his jerky movements had ripped the instrument from the transmission. By force of circumstance, he resorted to using drivers. First there was Tanios, a braggart from the Zgharta region, in northern Lebanon. Short-tempered by nature, he spent his time getting into fights. The day the first set of twins was born, my father received an urgent call from the Achrafieh police station in Beirut – Tanios had been arrested for firing a gun into the air from the roof of a building in celebration of the event ... The Admiral had to intercede with the prosecutor to ask that he go easy on this overly expressive man. The opposite of this Zghartian was Youssef, as gentle as a lamb, and fearful, so fearful that he did not insult the reckless driver who had nearly crashed into his car until he was a mile down the road, once he was sure he was out of his reach. There was also Abu Joseph, who spoke impeccable French; Jihad, who showed exemplary devotion and tuned in to wonderful radio shows; and then there was Salim, who came from the mountain city of Jezzine, in the southern part of the country, which he believed was the centre of the world, and who had raised nine children by the sweat of his brow.

On his way home, my father always gobbled down the apple quarters my mother had prepared for him in the morning and that he had not had time to eat at the office, then he would take a nap in the back seat. When the driver took the turn that led to our house, he would suddenly awaken, as if he had been warned by an invisible cuckoo clock or as if, in his dream, he had seen that he was almost home. When he came back from a high altitude, his ears were always blocked. It would take two or three hours for him to get his normal hearing back. This bothered me: the Admiral would talk loudly because he could not hear himself.

My father's office staff was his second family, and some days, when he was buried in a tricky case, it even seemed to us that it was his first. Among his assistants were Bilo, a lawyer who was as engaging as he was resourceful, and Simone, a faithful colleague from day one who translated all the English documents the Admiral received. For my father – have I mentioned this? – did not know Shakespeare's tongue (his vocabulary was limited to the expression 'fifty-fifty'), although he did legal work for two big American companies. There was also Antoine, faithful and dedicated, as meticulous as a bursar, who had spent his whole life at the office and had acquired enough experience to make even the most practised lawyer green with envy; Madame Doummar, the secretary, the Maginot Line, who filtered all calls and refused those that were undesirable *sine die*; then there was Camille, the handyman, who knew all of the clients' phone numbers by heart, but who was late every morning because he had had too much to drink the night before at the pub in Gemmayzeh. Though he had not had any schooling, he was unbeatable at crossword puzzles and filled in huge ones in his spare time. Any occasion a witness was needed for a deed, Camille volunteered and, sticking out his tongue to help him concentrate, affixed his signature to the bottom of the document. 'If I had received a pound for every signature,' he told me one day, 'I would own a building in Gemmayzeh by now!' Finally, there was a lawyer whose name I have forgotten and who had betrayed my father's trust – it was no doubt because of this man that the Admiral was always bitterly telling me he hated 'ungrateful people'; and Saleh, the clerk, who was a member of the small Jewish community in Beirut. At the beginning of the war, he had packed up and moved to New York, where his children had made their fortune. One evening, during heavy bombing, our telephone rang. It was Saleh. The call was ill-timed. Crouching down to avoid placing himself in the sight-line of the sniper on the rampage in the neighbourhood, the Admiral heard his old clerk say to him: 'Sorry to bother you, sir. I just wanted to tell you how much I admire you and that I haven't forgotten you!'

Friends

My father had many friends but, lacking time, he only saw them on rare occasions. First there were his classmates from the Jesuit junior high school: Ghosn, Gannageh, Safa, Margossian, Riga ... When he was with them, he reminisced about 'the good old days', the football games, the hikes. There were also his colleagues from law school: Mounir, Abdel-Basset, Kamal, Anis. A prominent lawyer, Anis made time for leisure activities, unlike my father who gladly sacrificed them on the altar of work. In his spare time, Anis went line fishing wearing a white sunhat and shorts, or enjoyed making ice-cream, which he handed out to friends and neighbours. My father also had client friends, those who, having spent so much time with him, had become attached to him. Among these was Elie, the head of a removals company. He had blue eyes and was balding. His face reflected his inner kindness. Elie was anxious, so anxious he called my father several times a day to ask for advice. The Admiral never complained about this, and, to reassure his friend, he always repeated the same thing: 'Don't worry, Elie. I'll take care of it. Turn on your television set and don't give it another thought!' To show his gratitude Elie always gave us for Christmas dozens of toys that a renowned American supplier sent to him, a certain Louis Marx, who had appreciated his hospitality during a trip to Lebanon. Then there was John. A former officer in the Fleet Air Arm of the Royal Navy who had made his home in Lebanon, he ran a prosperous shipping agency and, from time to time, wrote novels. His daughter, who spoke Arabic, had two cats, two pelicans and six dogs who, according to my father, were 'as big as camels'. Before going to visit her, the Admiral always took precautions and phoned half an hour before leaving, to give her enough time to tie up her 'camels'. There were also Georges, Fouad, Ida, Myrna, an elegant businesswoman with a passion for classical music, who admired the Admiral's rigour and appreciated his humour; Mr Capiomon, an old French friend; Aimée, whom he called 'the President' because she presided over the Baalbeck International Festival; and Tony, whose mother owned one of Beirut's grand hotels, which was destroyed during the war. Tony had left the country, in spite of my father's advice, to settle in Europe where he had married an Irishwoman. Thanks to occasional cease-fires, he sometimes came back to Lebanon and stayed with us. Every morning, the exuberant fifty-something-year-old man would slip on his tracksuit and play football with me in the garden. Finally there was Professor Tyan, a brilliant mind, a professor at the law school and a former Minister of Justice, who, although much older than the Admiral, enjoyed his company: sitting on the terrace, they were capable of spending three full hours discussing paragraph 2 of article 167 of the code of commerce with the same enthusiasm as a Juventus fan telling his colleagues about last night's game; and there was Father Emile, a colourful priest who, in reference to Don Camillo, went by the name of Don Emilio. To his parishioners, he prescribed 'laughing therapy' to combat 'doom and gloom' and freely cited this sentence from the Bible: 'A joyful heart is good medicine!' Don Emilio came to our house once a month and would spend the evening telling jokes. In spite of his busy schedule, my father listened to him with a smile and with admirable patience. To the ladies who reproached him for being voluble, Don Emilio would naively retort: 'It's normal: anyone in a gown is talkative!'

With his friends, my father sometimes 'let it all hang out': they would exchange hilarious anecdotes or launch into tall stories. One day, Anis paid him a visit along with a lawyer named Ramez. Ramez was fat, so fat that at hearings he took up half the bench reserved for the defence at the back of the court-room.

'I'll bet fifty pounds you're incapable of losing weight,' Anis challenged, taking my father as a witness.

'You're on!' the other responded.

'I'll give you two months to lose twenty pounds. If you

manage, I'll pay you fifty pounds; if you fail, you'll have to pay me!'

Then, turning towards my father: 'You'll be the arbitrator!'

Tempted by the idea, my father agreed and wrote a contract in due form on the spot, establishing the agreement of both parties.

Two months passed. Two months during which Anis, in order to 'corrupt' his opponent, invited him or had him invited to some twenty dinners in the city. The fateful day arrived. My father summoned Ramez and asked him to step onto the scales. The poor man complied with a heavy heart: rather than losing twenty pounds, he had gained four. Taking his role as arbitrator very seriously, the Admiral shut himself in his office and drew up a well-founded arbitral sentence in which, after the factual argument and a series of reasons adduced that were based on the Lebanese code of obligations and contracts, he upheld Ramez's liability while lightening it on the grounds of Anis's scheming, as he had knowingly contributed to his adversary's failure. So rather than the fifty pounds upon which they had agreed, Ramez was condemned to paying thirty to his friend. As soon as the arbitral sentence was pronounced, the latter claimed his due. Thinking it was a joke, Ramez rebuffed his request. Cut to the quick by this disloyal act, Anis went to the court-house and demanded that my father's sentence be executed. The judge in charge of the brief could not believe his eyes: he had certainly seen some crazy cases – cases involving stolen apples, poisoned cows or disturbances between neighbours caused by a rooster that crowed too early in the morning – but never had he had such an insane case submitted to him. He called Anis into his office: 'You're wasting my time!'

'I'm sorry, your Honour. This is an arbitral sentence like any other, pronounced by a star lawyer. If you reject my petition, I'll lodge a complaint for denial of justice!'

Taken aback, the judge ended up giving in and ruled that my father's sentence – ordering the obese party to pay thirty pounds to the other party for not having lost weight within the agreed time frame – be carried out. A first in legal history! After all was said and done, order was restored: afraid his furniture would be seized, Ramez agreed to pay the sum to Anis, who, proving to be a good sport, invited him ... to dinner.

Ping-pong

At the back of the garden under the arbour, there was a ping-pong table. In the summer, we played exciting matches with our friends there. When there were lots of us, we would rotate around the table, each holding a bat, taking turns hitting the ball. The player who missed the ball would step out of the game. One of my friends, Habib, had become a master of this art. Armed with a Stiga bat equipped with a 2.2 mm sponge and a long-pimple rubber sheet, he managed to outplay all his opponents thanks to precise strokes with unpredictable spin. Seeing him gesticulate, fidget, jump from one side of the table to the other, I sometimes found myself thinking that Darwinian theory was not unfounded.

One day, we organized a tournament in which all our cousins, friends and neighbours took part. After three hours of qualifying matches, with luck on my side, I made it to the final against Habib. I had a moment's hesitation:

up against a player of that calibre, I did not stand a chance. I would be better off forfeiting the game in order to leave the tournament with my head held high, avoiding looking ridiculous in front of my friends. My father, who was passing by, approached me. 'Go ahead, don't back out!' he said to me, patting me on the back. 'Don't forget: "Follow the leader!"'

I smiled. Emboldened, I took my position and began the match against a wrought-up Habib, all excited at the idea of winning the tournament. But three minutes later, a silly accident interrupted the match: I twisted my ankle while desperately trying to reach one of my opponent's balls, which had landed far in front of me, just inches from the net. The die was cast. Grimacing with pain, I began to walk towards Habib to congratulate him, when my father grabbed the bat from me and announced with his powerful voice: 'I'll take over!'

We thought he was joking. My friends looked at one another, dumbfounded. We had never seen my father play table tennis. Did he even know the rules of the game? Could he serve, do a backhand? As serious as could be, Father got in position, ready to serve. And the miracle occurred: he struck the ball against his bat with such force it was catapulted to the other end of the table at lightning speed. Habib did not even see it. He stood, mouth agape. Was it a stroke of luck? No. My father served four times in a row, and all four times his opponent was outplayed, incapable of intercepting the ball. Boosted by this advantage, Father won the game hands down, amidst applause. With a solemn gesture, he presented me with the little trophy. On his forehead, a 'v' formed: 'v' for victory.

Football

My father admired Pelé, Just Fontaine, Raymond Kopa, Platini and Eusebio. As a child, I used to watch football games with him on television. 'I'll take the guys in white, you take the guys in black,' he would say to me, taking care to choose the weaker team so I would have a chance of being on the winning side. He is the one who, in spite of his preference for track-and-field, introduced me to football and taught me the rules of the game. Later, my brothers, my cousins and I put together our own team, ambitiously baptized Dynamo Kleyate[1] in reference to Dynamo Kiev, the team that won the European Cup Winners' Cup in 1986. Though we were younger than our opponents, we won all our games thanks to our spirit of solidarity and our pugnacity. Our nicknames were borrowed from the great players of the time. I went by the name of Joe Jordan, like the Scottish centre forward. I was the team captain and set myself apart with my opportunism,

---

1. A Kesrouan village in the Lebanese mountains.

the orders I gave to my teammates and the frightful war cry I let out every time I scored a goal. Sometimes my sister would join us. She played under the name Trésor, like Marius, the player on the French national team. The best games of my life were played with those teammates, in spite of the hits we took, our opponents' cheating, refereeing errors and the fog that would take us by surprise in the middle of a game, so thick we could not make out our own players. As part of that team I learned patience, determination and the infinite joy that overtakes a player the moment the ball he has just shot goes into the opposing team's net.

My father never came to watch our games: too busy, he left it to my mother to accompany us in her immense Peugeot estate, which could hold the entire team (people would raise their eyebrows upon seeing eleven players get out of the car or pile into it). 'Mine' was more than a mother for us: she was a true coach, a sort of Guy Roux[1] in a skirt. She would get up early, wake us, distribute our uniforms and towels, tie our shoes, prepare the water bottles, load the bags into the car and then set off to collect the players. Having unloaded the team, she would watch the game from her car, parked near the football fields, listening to Vivaldi's *Four Seasons* on the car radio. When we scored a goal, she would honk the horn and flash the headlights to applaud the feat.

Upon our return, the Admiral would ask about the

---

1. A French football coach known for his paternalistic behaviour towards young players.

outcome, congratulate those who had scored, and console the losers. '*Laaébt mnih?*' (Did you play well?), '*Kam goal hotét?*' (How many goals did you score?) he would ask us enthusiastically. To earn his respect, we gave our all on the field.

Today, I have hung up my boots. I watch the games on television, my legs crossed on the coffee table, a glass of *arak* in hand. But every time I see a ball lying in the street or in a school playground, I cannot help but run up and shoot it. In homage to the Admiral.

Long Hair

'*Sar lazém t'oss chaarak!*'

My father ordered me to get a haircut every time he saw rebellious locks of hair encroaching onto my forehead. I hated – and still hate – going to the barber: that feeling of being at the mercy of his scissors, those hairs that creep inside your clothes, the hot blowing of the hairdryer ... Who can bear that? To push me to give in, Father would tease me: 'You're a *khanfouss*,'[1] or 'You look like Mireille Mathieu.'[2] Mireille Mathieu! Cut to the quick, I would comply without further discussion.

The village barber was a poor old man who had failed his junior high school exit exam seven times. The eighth time, the examination committee agreed to award him the diploma out of pity. The affair inspired a local poet: '*Sarlak sabeh snin*

---

1. What one calls a sheep with very curly wool.
2. A famous French singer from the 1970s known for her signature bowl cut.

hmar, hallak sar dawr el léjné, which means: 'You have been an ass for seven years, now the committee's turn has come!' Girgi – that was his name – gave everyone the same haircut, no matter who they were, and would incessantly abandon his customer – who was decked out in a pink apron, reminiscent of nursery school – in order to wait on other customers who entered his shop to buy cigarettes, a newspaper, a lottery ticket. Sometimes he even left to feed his goat that was tied to a stake outside, then came back to resume the haircut or shave. Sometimes my father escorted me all the way to the barber's to ensure that he would do a good job: 'Very short, especially around the ears, don't use the electric razor on his neck!' Having given his orders, he would wait, reading a newspaper. When the haircut was over, he would inspect my hair with an expert eye, patting my cheek with a satisfied look, pay, and walk me back to the house.

One day, while putting some photo albums away in the attic, I came across a picture of my father as a child. He must have been around ten years old and was posing next to his mother, wearing a suit with a sailor collar. I burst out laughing: he looked like Louis XIV as a child, with his hair cascading over his shoulders and a fringe lying across his forehead. I immediately went into his office, armed with the incriminating evidence.

'I demand an explanation, Father!' I said to him, with an ironic glint in my eye. 'You're the one who looked like Mireille Mathieu!'

He looked at the photograph, frowning as if he were having trouble recognizing the people in it. How could he have admitted to me that he had had long hair throughout his childhood?

'That's strange,' he mumbled, shrugging his shoulders. 'The barber must have been on holiday that week!'

The Chocolate Hunt

My father had a passion for chocolate. Who would have guessed that behind the austere lawyer there lay a man with a sweet tooth? To justify himself, he explained to me that Goethe never began a day without drinking a cup of hot chocolate, that cocoa beans were once called Theobroma, which means 'food of the Gods', and that in his book entitled *The Physiology of Taste*, the gastronome Brillat-Savarin observed that chocolate 'is very suitable for those who devote themselves to great intellectual efforts, to work in the pulpit, or to court-room work'.

In his law office, the Admiral readily gave out chocolates and sweets (he reserved mints for clients whose company he enjoyed, and caramels, which are more quickly swallowed, for talkative clients whose visits he hoped to cut short), but never cigarettes: he himself did not smoke, and, priding himself on having helped four of his friends give up smoking, he lectured the smokers he met, even if they were judges. He had an aversion to cigars: was it because they would stink up the room or because those who chewed on them had an unbearably conceited air about them? Sometimes, to show an employee that he was pleased with his work, he would call him into his office, open the cabinet behind him, and religiously pull out a box bearing the name Auer, Geneva confectioner 'for five generations', from which, with a solemn gesture, he would pull a piece of filled chocolate. The employee would take the offering, touched by this trivial yet highly symbolic token.

The youngest of the family, Fred Astaire, shared his taste for good things. Not satisfied with combing the kitchen for sweets – we credit him with the feat of having eaten thirty-six chocolate bars in a single day – he would occasionally sneak into our father's room, where no one dared go without permission, to unearth sweets. My father eventually noticed that his precious blue boxes – which were marked 'Marquise de Sévigné' and decorated with the bust of the famous letter writer – were the target of an elusive marauder whose identity he had deduced. He did not say anything to my brother, but he resolved to remove the chocolates from his greedy son's reach. Thus began a veritable game of hide-and-seek which, I must admit, sometimes took an absurd turn. My father put the box in a cupboard, which he double-locked and hid the key in the dresser: my brother found the key. He hid it amongst his shoes: Fred Astaire spotted it. He put it under his bed: the bandit easily unearthed and expertly looted it. This battle of wills went on for months without either of the adversaries openly bringing up the subject, as if, deep down, each of them was enjoying the game and feared that by talking about it, they would bring it to an end and dispel the mystery that surrounded it. Once, and only once, my father alluded to the game: while we were watching an animal documentary on television, he offered to let us each in turn choose a chocolate from his box. With the ease of a confectioner, he provided those who hesitated with precious details about the composition of each piece: 'this one is filled with delicate praline cream and coated with dark chocolate; that one is filled with raspberry liqueur without a sugar crust ...' When Fred Astaire's turn came, my father skipped over him. Dismayed, my youngest brother looked at him questioningly.

'You've already had your turn!' my father said to him, winking.

Hope

The war that ravaged Lebanon from 1975 to 1990 spared nothing: the country's infrastructure, economy, national unity, joie de vivre ... I remember terrible nights lit up by blazing fires, the deafening din of shells, the whistling of the snipers' bullets; I can still see the dead being transported in rubbish bags, the wounded being piled into ambulances, the refugees sleeping in parking lots, the car bombs, the devastated buildings, the crazed windows and the barricades; I can still smell the stench of blood, gunpowder, dust ... And I wonder how and why I came through it unscathed, though no one comes through such an ordeal completely unscathed.

During the war, my father, an optimist by nature, continued to make plans for the future, exhorted his friends not to jump ship, convinced that the 'good Lebanese people' had to stick together and not desert their own country. To those who, having lost everything, came to his house to bemoan the fact, he promised better days; he assured those who felt themselves giving in to despondency of a rapid end to the fighting; to those who wanted to take the path of exile, he explained that exile is not a remedy, but a poison. Was he himself sure of what he put forward, or was he bluffing in order to persuade them to stay? I think he felt he was invested with a national – almost divine – mission, which consisted of preaching hope: people arrived at his house discouraged, and left confident, without a care in the world.

One day when the bombs were raging, my mother came looking for him. She appeared very upset.

'What's going on?' he asked her.

'I'm afraid we'll have protesters in front of our house.'

My father frowned, went to the window and opened the curtains. 'Protesters? Who on earth would protest in front of our house?'

My mother shrugged her shoulders and retorted in a dead-pan tone: 'All the people you gave false hope to and who stayed in Lebanon because of you; all those you comforted and who are now hiding like rats to escape the bombs!'

My father always saw the good side of things, saw the glass half-full. He was so optimistic he had a very hard time imagining old age or death. At the age of seventy-three, he took offence at my classifying him as elderly. 'I'm not old,' he corrected me with a stern tone. And when my uncle died very suddenly, I can still see the Admiral full of hope in the car on the way to the hospital, incapable of imagining his brother dead. When we arrived at Accident and Emergency and Le Corbusier, in tears, told us it was over, my father remained lost for a few moments, looking distraught, his lips tensed.

'That's not possible,' he stammered, shaking me until my teeth rattled. 'They have to save him, it's not possible!'

'There's nothing more they can do, Father. He's gone.'

'It's not possible,' he repeated. 'It's not possible ...'

It was in fact possible. Death had taken my uncle, he who was goodness itself, he who, in a letter he had sent to Father, had written the following words: 'You are a father to us all; you are and will always be our last resort.'

Another day, during the most critical phase of the war, while we were in the bomb shelter, confined to the dark, foul-smelling room, attentive to the sound of the explosions that were shaking the city over our heads, we saw the Admiral arrive with a candle and a stack of files.

'What are you doing, Father?'

'I have files to get through,' he responded, settling into a corner of the shelter.

'What files? The country is devastated. There are no clients, no courts, no judges, no justice ... What's the use?'

My father nodded his head and spoke these magnificent words: 'Tomorrow peace will come, and I have to be ready.'

Nightmares

I can still see my father during the war. I have two unforgettable memories: the shells raining down on our house, and us, huddled in a junk room, not daring to breathe. The Admiral is deadly pale; for the first time, he is afraid. Afraid for us. He knows he can no longer protect us. That only Providence can still save us.

Another time, taking advantage of a lull, we cross a roadblock to inspect our house, which we have abandoned due to the violence of the internecine fighting between General Aoun's men and the Lebanese Forces. We zigzag around the mines. A sentry stops us and, in an unpleasant tone, asks my father for his papers. Father digs through his pockets in search of his ID card. The militiaman has red hair, his skin is covered in freckles. How old is he? Barely eighteen. In normal times, he would be at school preparing for his baccalaureate exam. His combat uniform is hanging off him, his boots are too big.

'*Khallessna ba'a*! Hurry up!'

The militiaman is losing patience, he raises his voice. I bite my lip: if the situation turns ugly, how will we be able to defend Father? We are unarmed, harmless, but obviously our innocence does not suffice. My father clenches his fists; his jaw tightens. I can tell he would like to smack this idiot once or twice but, thank God, he regains his self-control. This scene where a boy, wet behind the ears, takes the liberty of bullying the Admiral comes back to me often. It shows the extent to which war respects nothing. Neither the dead, nor the living.

Hit by thirteen shells, occupied in turn by the warring parties, our house suffered during the war. Tank tracks churned up the garden, crushed the flowers and ripped up the trees – with the exception of the cedar, which was too resilient. The arbour and the ping-pong table were crushed; the orchard and the vegetable garden transformed into trenches. I can still see my father, his hands on his hips, standing in the middle of this lunar landscape. The pallor of his face conveys his sorrow. What had they done to his paradise? In the name of what cause did they destroy it? On the walls, the militiamen left graffiti glorifying their leader:

> *Talama hounaka noujoum fil sama'*
> *Satabka hikayat al-Hakim wal kouwwat*!

As long as there are stars in the sky

The epic of the *Hakim*[1] and the Lebanese forces
shall live!

The militiamen were poets.

'Uncontrolled elements' of the army, those referred to as
'*al-aanasser ghaïr al-moundabita*', took advantage of the
reigning anarchy to pillage our house. They took their time,
inspected the cupboards, explored the attic, packed up the
furniture, sipped from a glass, smoked a cigarette, defecated
in the living room, then loaded their booty onto covered
trucks. Nothing disrupted their work. I came across the
inventory of stolen objects my mother had drawn up:

> A Caucasian rug.
> Three candlesticks.
> A carved wood mirror.
> A small embroidered tablecloth.
> A salmon platter.
> A Limoges china sweet dish.
> Two lacquered Chinese chairs.
> An Amin Sfeir painting of the six children ...

The pillagers had good taste.

---

1. 'The Doctor'. The nickname given to the leader of the
Lebanese Forces, Samir Geagea.

The Tragedy

Night is falling on Beirut. The muezzin's voice and the cathedral bells call to one another. The shops lower their metal shutters with a crash. Peace has returned, but joie de vivre has not. The rebuilding of Lebanon is an illusion: a shattered vase whose pieces have been glued back together bears its cracks for ever. The atmosphere is oppressive. Is it the heat, or the sensation of being permanently on reprieve in this country sitting on a volcano?

'I have something important to tell you.'

My father looks tired. He hangs his lawyer's gown in the wardrobe, enters the living room and collapses into his armchair.

'I'm listening, Father.'

He looks at me fixedly. In his eyes, I see an unfamiliar hint of sadness.

'I'll soon be leaving.'

'Where are you going?'

'An accident can so easily happen. A blood clot, an embolism ...'

'I don't like it when you talk to me about these things; you know that, Father.'

It is true: I do not like him to talk to me about death. It is not that the evocation of the Reaper is difficult for me – I lived through fifteen years of the Lebanon War, and during that time death dominated my thoughts – but I cannot imagine, not even for an instant, my father's death.

'I need to talk to you,' he continues, pressing my hand. 'If I go, I'm counting on you.'

'You can always count on me!'

I bend over him to kiss him on the forehead. His hand clasps the nape of my neck.

Two days later, at the office, around noon, while I am putting some paperwork away in my desk, my father's cry rings out. He calls to me, asks me to help him. I run to him. An intern and the secretary are there. The Admiral is sitting down, but he is grimacing with pain.

'Ouch, it hurts here, in my back!'

The secretary takes the situation lightly. She thinks it is a cramp, brings him a glass of water and an aspirin.

'To the hospital!' I say firmly.

I know that things are serious: General de Gaulle died this way.

'Should we call an ambulance?' the secretary asks.

'There's no time, we'll drive him there!'

In the lift, my father can hardly stand up. He is pale and tense. I have never seen him in such a state. I do my best to hold him up. We get into the car. I take his hand, he squeezes it so hard it hurts. The driver shoots off towards the nearest hospital, honking. We go into Accident and Emergency. They put my father in a wheelchair and give him an electro-cardiogram. The intern is categorical: it is a heart attack. They take him into the examination room. Ten minutes later, the cardiologist comes out to talk to me: 'We have to operate immediately. There's not a moment to lose!'

I feel my hands and legs trembling. What I had feared would happen is happening.

'What is it?'

'Aortic dissection.'

'Is it serious, Doctor?'

'The operation entails replacing the aorta with a Dacron prosthesis, putting in place an aortic valve prosthesis, and reimplanting the coronary arteries ...'

His explanations are beyond me.

'What are his chances of pulling through?'

'One in three.'

While the surgeons are preparing in the operating theatre, we are all here, Mama, my brothers, my sister and I. United, the way he has always wanted it. What shocks us is that this accident was unexpected. My father has never had an operation, has never undergone treatment for anything. His medical exams, at the age of eighty, were like those of a young man. Nothing, aside from his confession the other night, led us to expect this 'aortic dissection' whose name alone gives me the shivers. This incident has confirmed my belief that most people know when their time has come, and organize their departure as artists or athletes do at the end of their career: Mozart himself apparently saw the *Requiem* as a premonition of his upcoming death. Deep down, I have always been an instinctive person: I believe in love at first sight, in signs, in voices that come from within or from above. It is what Kahlil Gibran called 'the third eye', the one that sees the invisible. I am convinced that my father knew.

Nine hours later, the surgeons come out of the operating theatre, dishevelled, drenched with perspiration.

'So, Doctor?'

'He'll live, but there will be after-effects. We had to make a choice: continue with the operation or give up. We preferred to continue.'

Two days later, I am authorized to see my father in the recovery room. Wearing a green hospital gown that buttons down the back and a protective cap, I walk towards him. He is lying on a bed with tubes coming out of his nose and mouth, and his cheeks are hollow. Under the blanket, he is naked. I jump: I have never seen my father naked. His chest rises: he is breathing, and that is what matters. Will he recognize me? I speak to him. He opens his eyes and nods his head. Yes, he recognizes me. He takes my hand and squeezes it hard, very hard, as if he were clinging to it.

After-effects

The after-effects the doctor spoke of did appear: partial paralysis, aphasia. Aphasia? The word takes my breath away. Aphasia! How would my father be able to bear this situation, he who, in court or with his clients, spent his whole life pleading or talking; he who, as a child, was so talkative that he was always put between the Safa brothers, two very well-behaved classmates; he who, at table, monopolized the conversation and tirelessly talked to us about Sacha Guitry or Flaubert and his five rough drafts! An irony of sorts: the Admiral no longer has a voice, is enclosed in silence. How can I forgive God for having taken the ability to speak away from my father? How can I accept the idea that there is a good and just God when He condemns a good and just man to silence? My mother does not share my anger. She says that saints have always suffered.

I close my eyes: I already miss the tone of his voice, the way he clears his throat, his affectionate words ... What indescribable frustration there is in seeing a loved one without being able to hear what he has to say to us! My father has always been an example for me, a role model, even when he was tough with me, uncompromising, even when we were not on the same wavelength, undoubtedly because of the half-century that lay between us. My pain is immeasurable. But I have to resign myself. At his age, at eighty, cells no longer regenerate. Force of will and doctors serve no purpose. My only consolation is that he is still with us, fully conscious, surrounded by his loved ones.

I go up into the Admiral's bedroom to put his things away. I dread this moment: I do not like to invade people's privacy; I look like a poacher venturing into forbidden territory. His pen, his watch, his wallet, his lawyer's card, his address book are there. On his desk, a sheet of paper where he wrote his weekly schedule. He crossed out the things he had already done with a red pen. I carefully fold it and slip it into my pocket: I have to continue what he started. I lie down on his bed and bury my head in his pillow: his scent is still there. At my feet, there is a pair of slippers I used to like to wear to imitate him. On a shelf, between the Napoleon statuette and the book on Lyautey, which he had been awarded for excellence in history at the Jesuit school, there is a photo album: there he is as a child, with his long hair, or as a teenager, dressed up as

Richelieu. There is also a picture of him crouching down beside me in front of a huge Dodge, and the black and white photo of him wearing a suit and tie, standing in front of Saint Peter's Basilica in Rome, his back straight, his hands behind his back, his legs spread slightly apart. My father looks like a film star in this picture, like a 'leading man' as he used to say, laughing. In a file, I find the arbitral sentence he had pronounced in the case of Anis v. Ramez, and the promise, signed by his own hand, to take Mama to Venice. In the end, destiny has not given him the chance to keep his promise. In another file, I find all of my French compositions, lovingly kept in a nylon folder, and the manuscript of 'Bob on a Cruise', a copy of which he had secretly obtained from my mother. The fact that my father has kept these documents brings tears to my eyes. In a little notebook, there are two quotations, which he had carefully copied in black ink. The first is from 'If', Kipling's famous poem:

> If you can ... watch the things you gave your life
>   to broken,
> And stoop and build 'em up with worn-out
>   tools.
> ...
> And lose, and start again at your beginnings
> And never breathe a word about your loss;
> ...
> you'll be a Man, my son!

The other is from Blaise Pascal: 'The greatest charity we can show towards the dead who are dear to us is to do what they would have wished us to do while they were still alive.'

In a small transparent box, there is a lock of hair. I take it and, in front of the mirror that hangs on the wall, I compare it with my own hair. The colour is the same.

The Admiral's Song

Months pass. My father has returned home. We surround him with our affection. His morale is good, especially when he goes to his 'paradise', his country house, restored after the fighting ended. Sometimes I push his wheelchair out onto the balcony where we used to take moonlight walks, his hand gently encircling the nape of my neck. We follow the same path, back and forth, contemplating the moon, open like a huge eye. I rest my hand on the nape of his neck: just like his gesture. He savours the moment. I replay our common memories. I thank God for having kept him by our side for such a long time, he who married late in life. Two of my friends were not so lucky: both lost their fathers too soon during the war, and suffered terribly from this premature departure. I think of the good times spent with him, and of the bad times as well. I better understand his constant dissatisfaction, his desire to see us base our own way of life on his. I understand now that this attitude was not at all selfish, rather that it was dictated by his desire to incite us to surpass ourselves, to give the very best of ourselves, to be men, quite simply. Deep down, being a father is a thankless job. Who can judge one's father, understand his motives, measure the sacrifices he has made or guess the problems he has secretly had to face? The image of the merciful father in the biblical parable of the prodigal son is indeed touching, but what can we say about the 'prodigal fathers', those who leave one day and come up against a wall of incomprehension upon their return?

Sometimes, during our moonlight stroll, the Admiral lifts his face to the sky. He looks out into space, at the stars, where everything is silence. Is he yearning for the moment of his departure? Is he waiting for the final signal? I kiss his hand. Stay, Father, stay! The absence of your voice is nothing compared to your presence. And the love we read in your eyes is stronger than the silence that has sealed your lips.

Every morning, my father lets the nurse shave him. He puts as much care into this shaving ritual as he did before, when he was in full possession of his faculties: he shows the 'barber' the spots that are poorly shaven, with a hand gesture shows him how to proceed, scolds him if he does not do his work properly. But the Admiral no longer sings: neither 'Padam' nor 'Catari' ring out in the bathroom any more.

At nine o'clock, he receives communion from the hands of Bouna Hanna (Don Emilio is no longer of this world). Then, with the help of a physiotherapist, he does his exercises, which are meant to help him stay in shape, to prevent the paralysis from taking over his other limbs. Observing him, I recall our physical education sessions; I admire his perseverance, his determination, his patience: even in this state, he has not given up the hope he has always advocated. Deep down, it is not so much professional success that constitutes the Admiral's greatness as his capacity to face all hardships with courage.

A young speech therapist takes over next: she teaches him to articulate better, to separate syllables, to pronounce his words in a more intelligible manner. Without conviction, he plays this game that reduces him to the level of a four-year-old child. He knows it will not do any good. It is too late.

In the afternoon, my mother reads books to him – de Gaulle, always – he watches Sacha Guitry and Fernandel videos, but not Harry Baur videos, which are too hard to find. The courts and cases? Henceforth all that is far away, very far. When I tell him about the problems the lawyers at the court-house are having, he unclenches his teeth as if to exclaim: 'What a terrible shame!' Yes, Father, what a terrible shame. Nothing has changed since your forced retirement. Often, I wonder: 'What would he have done in my place? What would he have said? How would he have written this contract, pleaded this case?' My father inhabits me. His figure, even silent, reassures me.

Since his accident, he no longer likes to receive guests. Only Anis, Mounir, Samir, Abdel-Basset, Salim and Antoine come regularly to keep him company and to tell him funny stories which trigger silent laughter. Why not his other friends? He probably prefers to leave those who admire him with the image of a man in full possession of his faculties, the image of the Admiral.

At dusk we sing the canticles of the month of Mary before the photograph of the Virgin of Harissa – this photograph he loves, a representation of the Virgin with the moon as her halo. And it is at that moment that, every evening, the miracle occurs:

> *Ave,*
> *Ave,*
> *Ave Maria!*

My father's voice rises from the very depths of his being. A melodious voice, clear and in tune. We hear it, finally, this voice that we miss, just for the duration of this sacred song. And then, once again, silence falls upon the Admiral.

Epilogue

I knew freedom was contagious. In Martyrs' Square, a large crowd has gathered on this day, 14 March 2005, exactly one month after the assassination of Prime Minister Rafik Hariri. How many of us are there, the Lebanese people who have come out into the streets to demand the departure of the Syrian troops that have been occupying the country for thirty years? Maybe a million: one in four citizens! Never in the history of Lebanon have the people mobilized in such a way. My mother is here; I squeeze her hand: I cannot lose her. She, like me, senses that she is taking part in a crucial event. But does she even consider the dangers that threaten us? A single gunshot fired into the air could spread panic. Next to us, an older woman is agitated. She is euphoric, her hair is in disarray, she is wearing a red and white scarf. With a cheerful voice, she chants: '*Horrié, siadé, istiklal*' (Freedom, sovereignty, independence!). I look around me: the young are mixing with the old; the poor with the rich; Christians with Muslims. A teenager sitting on his friend's shoulders is waving the Bible in one hand, the Qur'an in the other. A young girl with green eyes has a sticker on her forehead that says 'Independence 05'. A celebratory atmosphere reigns in Beirut. Who will find this surprising? Celebration has always been the driving force of revolutions: the sans-culottes sang while storming the Bastille. Further on, on the platform, there is one speaker after another: Marwan Hamadeh, Samir Frangieh, Nayla Moawad, Samir Kassir ... The journalist Gebran Tueni[1] makes the following vow, taken up in unison by the crowd:

> *Nouqssimou bil lahi al-azim*
> *Mousslimina wa massihiyin*
> *Ann nabka de iman mouahaddin*
> *Il al-abadi al-abidin*
> *Difa'aan aan Loubnan al-Azim!*

> We swear by Almighty God
> Muslims and Christians
> To remain forever united
> For centuries and centuries
> For the defence of glorious Lebanon!

Near the Martyrs' statue, only recently returned to its proper location, tents have been set up. Students have decided to take possession of this symbolic place and to refuse to evacuate it until the Syrian troops have departed. Like a challenge. The Lebanese soldiers in charge of maintaining order observe the protesters

---

1. In 2005, Samir Kassir and Gebran Tueni paid for their commitment to freedom with their lives.

with complicity: they have been demanding the very same thing for a long time. In the crowd, I spot my brothers and my sister. The whole tribe is here. Leonardo is waving the Lebanese flag, white for hope, red for blood, with a cedar in the middle.

'If Father sees us on television, he'll be happy,' my brother says to me. 'It'll be like he's here with us, taking part in the event!'

I nod my head. My father had been waiting for the day of liberation for thirty years. But when the day finally came, he was no longer able to get around, to come out into the streets. What does it matter, anyway? Right now, with his eyes glued to the television set, he must be thinking he was right to preach hope.

In the evening, I eat at my parents' house. My father's tastes have changed: he no longer likes fruit, and eats very little chocolate.

'Do you remember, Father, what you said to the notary one day?'

He smiles, his cheeks dimple. Yes, he remembers. That day, he had gone to the notary's office for a formality. The notary, who knew that our country house had been ravaged by thirteen bomb shells and that all of the trees in the garden – with the exception of the cedar – had been flattened, had declared to my father, sounding distressed: 'My condolences, sir. It was with great sadness that I learned your house had been destroyed. What a tragedy.'

Lifting his index finger, my father replied: 'Yes, but the cedar is still standing!'